MW01204680

# SURVIVING
## Stolen Innocence

## BY ALICIA L. BROWN

Copyright © 2016 by Alicia L. Brown

*Surviving Stolen Innocence*
by Alicia L. Brown

Printed in the United States of America.

ISBN 9781498464079

All rights reserved solely by the author. The author guarantees all contents are orig-
inal and do not infringe upon the legal rights of any other person or work. No part of
this book may be reproduced in any form without the permission of the author. The
views expressed in this book are not necessarily those of the publisher.

Unless otherwise indicated, Scripture quotations taken from the New King James
Version (NKJV). Copyright © 1982 by Thomas Nelson, Inc. Used by permission.
All rights reserved.

www.xulonpress.com

# TABLE OF CONTENTS

# Acknowledgements

To God, for always protecting, blessing, and restoring me on a daily basis. Because of Your love, I am able to love. Because of life's pain, trials, tribulations, and blessings, I know how to not only survive, but also thrive. Thanks.

To my parents, James E. and Veronica C. McCoy, for your love, prayers, and support since birth. No matter what I need, though not much, you are always there. Thanks.

To my siblings, Al Brown and Vernicia Washington, for being supportive, uplifting, and great servants of God. I am grateful you never let me quit on self, family, others, and life. Thanks.

To my friend, "King," for listening, encouraging, and supporting me since the day I met you. Your contribution to my life is priceless. Thanks for your wisdom, knowledge, friendship, and daily prayers. I am humbled in your presence. Thanks!

To my "Care Bears," Malachi and Caleb Washington and Gabriella and Hannah Brown, for being the little angels God sent to shower me with love, joy, and wisdom each time you are in my presence. I love you and know God has ordered your little footsteps to become prosperous and successful in all you do.

To my entire family, for always being supportive, loving, prayerful, and for showering me with words of encouragement. I am grateful for what you do and have done for me. I love you and am forever humbled and thankful to be a part of a close-knit, loving family. Thanks.

To my editor, Claudia Moss, my former high school English teacher, editor of my Master's Thesis, mentor, friend, and author of *If You Love Me, Come: a novel*, *The Wanda B. Wonders series: a short story collection,* and *Soft Tsunami: poetry.* Because she asked me to submit a personal testimony of surviving rape to her anthology, I was able to give birth to this book. Your stern encouragement fueled my determination to overcome my fear of writing then and now. I appreciate you for challenging me to step out on faith with this project. Thanks.

To Jennifer Key, owner of Keys to a Healthy Relationship, for counseling, empowering, and encouraging me to complete this book before the end of 2015. I DID IT! Thanks.

To my cousins, Darnicia E. Turner, author of *The Music Within Me*, and Candy J. Rogers Prosper, owner of Best Days Counseling, for advice, wisdom, and encouragement throughout this project. Thanks.

# DEDICATION

This book is dedicated to the countless children, women, and men who were courageous in surviving stolen innocence to include, but not limited to, sexual, psychological, physical, and substance abuse. I salute you for finding your strength to survive. I encourage you to share your testimony. You never know who has experienced a similar situation and needs encouragement to escape. Free yourself and LIVE LIFE in a healthy way! I survived, and so can you. We are all worthy of surviving.

# PREFACE

Greetings friends!

My name is Alicia L. Brown, aka "Shawn." I am a native of Atlanta, Georgia, where I have resided since birth within a large, blended family. One of eight children, I am blessed to have a family who gives love, support, and respect endlessly and effortlessly. I have a host of nieces and nephews, whom I call my "Care Bears," and I have one goddaughter, whom I helped groom into a beautiful young woman. My "Care Bears" and goddaughter are the children God gave me to help raise.

Earning a 4.0 G.P.A., I graduated from Strayer University in Marietta, Georgia, with a Master's in Public Administration. I currently work for a state government organization utilizing my education, prior work experiences, and years of service in local faith and community-based non-profits to ensure procurement and payment integrity.

I am a servant of God, who is passionate about serving His people in whatever capacity He instructs me to do so and at the appointed time. I accepted Christ at the age of 11 years old. I served in various ministries and held positions such as Vice President of the Youth Usher Board, Assistant Youth Leader, Youth Event Coordinator, Assistant Athletic Director, Athletic Board Member, and teacher. Serving in these ministries led me to develop a daily prayer life and opened the way for me to meet several leaders and philanthropists in the community. I love praying, praising and worshipping God, and sharing my numerous testimonies as often as I can. Lastly, I am a philanthropist, who loves giving my time and monetary gifts to non-profits and people in need.

This book is one of my gifts to the world. I wrote it to shine the light of encouragement and love on all those who suffer in silence.

## The Stolen Innocence

In 1979, a 5-year-old girl was playing on the playground with her classmates, cousins, and brother. The summer air was filled with laughter. Her playmates having run off, from her seat on the see-saw, she noticed an older boy beckoning invitingly for her to come to him. Although she didn't know he was 13 years old and harboring ill intent, she stared curiously, though hesitantly, for a long time, until he asked if she wanted to see his dog. When she approached the teenager, he grabbed her arm tightly and told her to shut up. She screamed, but her little voice was drowned under waves of laughter. The boy managed to drag her off the playground as she desperately looked at her brother and cousins, hoping they saw her being dragged off her safe haven...or so she thought. Less than a yard from the playground, he dragged her into the woods. He put a log against her throat to threaten her, if she didn't obey. He snatched her hair bows from her plaits and pulled her pants down. She fought as much as she could. As her innocence was being stolen, the thief growled, "If you tell, I will kill you and your family!" In the distance, she heard adults calling her name after approximately four or five minutes. The sound of their voices and footsteps neared, becoming louder, closer. Thankful, she lay on the ground motionless, grateful the monstrous act was over. In spite of her horrific experience, she managed to identify the teenage beast when he boldly returned to the playground the next day. Her bravery prompted her to provide the local police department with a statement. Because of her bravery, the teenager was apprehended.

## The Surviving Stolen Innocence Begins

I am the little girl in the story. It has been over 30 years since that incident occurred and 20 years since I shared the story at a Christian women's retreat, where the guest speaker shared how she fought to overcome the scares and emptiness from a similar experience.

At a retreat meeting, approximately 20 women shared their testimonies of going from victim to victor. Women from all walks of life spoke one after another. The room was filled with weeping as a sign of relief. Other women yelled praises to God for saving and healing them. A handful of women informed the audience that their abusers were identified, apprehended, and convicted. Unfortunately, some of their abusers were fathers, family members, boyfriends, and women.

As I looked around the room, my heart was burdened with the desire to share my story. Prior to attending the retreat, I'd debated whether or not to tell my story but was detoured by the uncertainty of how others would view me, especially my mother and two godmothers. Embarrassment, lack of self esteem, and self worth kept me silent.

After the meeting ended, I prayed and asked God to help me to release my story so I could begin the healing process and experience the freedom and womanhood about which other women spoke. I saw peace, happiness, and joy in their eyes, heard it in their voices, and felt it in their warm embrace. I knew I was well beyond being in the dark. Although I wore a warm, beautiful smile on my lips and my eyes sparkled, I felt worthless on the inside. "God, help me to become a Proverbs 31 Woman" was my heart's desire and my new life mantra. Finally, I was ready to let go and let God.

# INTRODUCTION

I n 2001, my brother announced to our church that he had gotten engaged. What a surprise to me! Of course, my emotions were all over my face. I couldn't fake a smile. Observing the reaction of the congregation, I saw people rejoicing, dancing, and shouting, "Congratulations, Minister Al!" Try as I might to be a supportive sister and more so, a fellow youth leader, I began asking myself, "Why am I not happy? Why am I not rejoicing? Am I mad? If so, why am I mad? At whom am I angry? What is going on inside me, preventing me from celebrating a major event in my brother's life?" I did not have the answers, but I knew God did.

As soon as church dismissed, I darted to the parking lot. All I wanted to do was get into my car, drive home, and cry, but before I reached the parking lot, a couple of the youth members saw me and asked me how I felt about the news. One of them said, "Ms. Shawn, your feelings are all over your face! Are you okay?" I nodded, but on the inside, I was far from okay. Perhaps I lied knowing I needed to appear supportive of my brother, though I did not know how to be so in that moment. I only knew I was in turmoil and needed to get to a happy, healthy place within myself, if I aimed to uncover the root cause of my brewing negative emotions. I needed help. ASAP!

A few steps from my car door, two other ministers stopped me. I wondered what they wanted. Somehow I hoped they could see that I wasn't in the mood to talk right then, but one spoke emphatically, "Get over yourself! Your face says it all! You ain't hiding from no one!" How true! If it weren't for my sunglasses and the Holy Spirit,

I am quite sure I'd have given them an unkind look and hard words. They should have perceived I was not in the mood for judgment, critiques, or unsolicited advice. However, with practiced discipline, I kept it together, held my tongue and eventually acknowledged them. In a strange sense, I wanted to know where this untimely conversation or intervention was leading.

One minister must have sensed the heat rising from my flesh because she took a different technique for addressing me. She asked me to walk with her to the recreation center next door. On the two-minute walk, she said, "I know you're emotional. I gathered from your reaction you did not know your brother was going to announce his engagement. I could tell you felt ambushed. After observing your body language, I knew I had to I get to you quickly. Before I left the sanctuary, I spoke briefly with your brother and mother. They informed me you were not told beforehand." She drew a deep breath and then continued speaking. "I expressed to them by keeping you out of the loop, you became an outsider, which you have felt your entire life. She looked into my eyes, while hers filled with concern. "I am recommending you attend counseling classes at another church so you can work through this. I'm a participant, and it has helped me." She glanced around for paper and something to write with. On the back of a flyer she found on a small table, she wrote an address in an elegant script. "Meet me here tomorrow. It's time you became a Proverbs 31 Woman. Get your healing today."

Later that night, I pondered on the events that occurred earlier in the day. The conversation with the minister was on replay in my mind. "Get your healing" rang loudly in my ears, convicting my heart. What, I wondered, had caused the whirlwind of emotions? Achieving wholeness and total healing were my focus. Being a supportive sister to my brother and now, to my future sister-in-law, was my end goal. I prayed and fasted for the remainder of that day. Unsure of my next steps, I asked God if the counseling classes were His plans for my healing. The next day, God revealed His answer. *Yes, go! It's for you!*

The following day, on Monday evening, I arrived at the church the minister had recommended. I was excited and ready to begin my healing journey. I listened attentively to the speakers as they described the different types of counseling classes. The church was multiracial, which was refreshing. As I sat in the audience, I could feel the spirit of humbleness and love. During the welcome period, an usher greeted me with a much-needed hug. She handed me a program of free, community classes.

As I browsed the program, I saw two interesting classes: Overcomers: Weight Loss Program and Adult Children: Dysfunctional Family. My minister friend suggested the latter, but I wasn't quite sure if it was really for me. Again, of course, I prayed about it, and as God would have His way, by 8 p.m. that night, He revealed which class I was to attend.

After the introduction of classes and opening prayer, a young white married couple appeared on the stage to share their testimony about the Adult Children: Dysfunctional Family Program. The wife shared how the class helped her to become a whole woman able to truly love her husband without fear of rejection, infidelity, and divorce. Her husband shared how the class helped him overcome scars from childhood abuse, which he'd suppressed for years. He recognized he needed help when he and his wife had their first argument. He became so angry he yelled at her, his angst resulting in him almost hitting her. Not wanting a dysfunctional marriage like his parents, he sought help. He wanted to love his wife like Christ loved the church. As he spoke, his voice broke and he lowered his head. Once he composed himself, he apologized to his wife and asked for her forgiveness. He knew his wife shouldn't have to bear the brunt of his dark past.

The husband's testimony registered in my spirit. I knew I needed to be delivered from the dark days of my childhood. His testimony prompted me to enroll in the Adult Children's program immediately. Prior to hearing this testimony, I had been afraid to seek help. The fear of embarrassment held me prisoner within myself. Something about that testimony gave me an incredible amount of strength and bravery to work on my healing and freedom from the scars of my innocence being stolen at five years of age.

During orientation, the counselor assured us that this program was not about others. It was not to embarrass anyone. It was not to make us feel guilty. It was about healing. It was about allowing God to heal us beyond the hurt. He also stated the counseling session was a two-year, self-paced program.

Regardless of the time frame, healing was my end goal. I wanted to be able to love myself so I could love my family and others like Christ loves me.

# Chapter 1

## ADMISSION

The first step in healing is admitting there is a problem. I could admit there was a problem, but could not pinpoint the exact problem. At the beginning of the group counseling session, the counselor informed the group the topic was fear. We had to identify and share a fear, past or current. As seen in the movies, we sat in a circle to share our experiences. In my mind, I determined that I was going to say that I had no fear, but the Holy Spirit had a different plan.

When my mouth opened, the Holy Spirit said, "I fear my brother is going to leave me like our daddy did, and I will be alone again." Hearing my words, I was shocked. What the what! That was not to have been my response! The counselor asked me what brought about this fear. The Holy Spirit responded, "He recently got engaged." And there it was. The root of my tsunami of emotions at church the day my brother announced his engagement. Fear had moved into my heart, and its eviction had to be now.

The Holy Spirit did His job of revealing truth. Now, it was on me to do the work. I determined that I was going to buckle down, swallow my pride, forget about what others thought, and press through the pain to achieve wholeness.

After the first session ended, the group recited the Serenity Prayer below.

## The Serenity Prayer

God grant me the serenity
To accept the things I cannot change;
Courage to change the things I can;
And wisdom to know the difference.
Living one day at a time;
Enjoying one moment at a time;
Accepting hardships as the pathway to peace;
Taking, as Jesus did, this sinful world
As it is, not as I would have it;
Trusting that He will make all things right
If I surrender to His Will;
So that I may be reasonably happy in this life
And supremely happy with Him
Forever and ever in the next.
Amen.

When I arrived home that night, I felt a heavy weight had been lifted from my chest. I recited the Serenity Prayer over and over, and under the power of the Words, I felt tears stream down my face. It was a sign of a breakthrough. I was finally able to admit I had a problem. The fear of my brother leaving me was the root cause of my suppressed, negative emotions. Fear was preventing me from being truly happy on the inside for my brother. It disfigured my face and darkened my day.

Yet the fear of my brother leaving me was a partial truth. Remember, the Holy Spirit had spoken on my behalf, revealing my brother leaving me like our biological father had was my issue, but being alone again was my whole truth. I needed to know why I was afraid of being alone, so I asked God to show me the truth.

Before my fifth birthday, my biological father died. My mom was left to raise my brother and me as a single parent. My brother and I, thirteen months apart in age, became closer at the news of our father's death. Throughout our lives, we were always together. I clung to him every chance I could. Subconsciously, I had assigned him the roles of my new protector, provider, and best friend, and before long, he took the place of our father in my life.

Because our family instilled in us to protect each other, I knew I had to protect him as well. My mother was extremely protective of us, especially after what happened to me on the playground a year later. For the next ten years, the three of us were always together and protecting each other. This was my life and all I knew, so the thought of being alone terrified me.

In my mind and heart, my brother's engagement and upcoming marriage was equivalent to my biological father's absence in my life. His absence in my home was a very fearful experience. I did not know how to cope with this reality. Fear hindered me from seeing the good side of my brother's engagement and distanced me from the joy of having a new sister. With the help of group counseling sessions and me doing the work, my fear slowly vanished. I was ready to welcome and embrace my sister-in-law.

Admission was my first step in surviving stolen innocence. It afforded me the opportunity to know the root causes of my fear. And, it brought me a new level of freedom. Facing this truth and sharing it in a group positioned me to accept that my long-ago rape had occurred; however, I did not have to remain embarrassed or afraid. The healing had begun.

# Chapter 2

# ACCEPTANCE

A ccepting the fact that my sexual innocence had been stolen was a difficult task. It required me to stand in front of a mirror as if I were confronting the thief. I stood in the mirror for hours, yet I could not tell myself the rape had occurred. I did not want to recall that moment. From the time I shared my story at the Christian women's retreat to this point was almost 10 years. I'd blocked the rape from my mind. Now, no longer willing to deny it had happened and desiring to release its vise hold on me, I stared into the mirror as long as it was required to speak the words.

As I looked at my reflection, I was finally able to recall the hidden image. I remembered seeing myself enjoying a fun time with my brother, cousins, and classmates on a playground, which had been my safe haven. I knew again the feeling of being dragged off the playground. Once more, I heard this monster threatening to kill my family and me.

Then the vision faded, and feelings of hurt, rage, emptiness, fear, disgust, and loneliness overcame me. Vengeance was present, too. I wanted to do bodily harm to the boy, I wanted to protect other children from him, and I wanted his mother to feel the pain my mother and I felt. Most importantly, I wanted revenge.

With the help of group counseling sessions and praying John 4:24,"…The truth shall make you free," I was not only able to accept that the assault had taken place, but I also accepted it on different levels. I was able to accept that it was not my fault. I was able to accept the teenage perpetrator was temporarily possessed with a spirit of sexual immorality. I was able to accept he was not in his right mind at the time he snatched my innocence. I was able to accept he was probably a victim of sexual abuse. And I was able to accept he needed healing and deliverance from his unclean ways.

Acceptance allowed me to pray for the young man's soul. I asked God to deliver him from the spirit of rape, molestation, and other similar spirits that caused him to rape little girls. I even recall writing a letter to him detailing my feelings towards him. I wanted the teenager to know that he had stolen something sacred and pure, something I could never regain! I told him I forgave him as well. After I read the letter aloud, I shredded it as a sign of complete closure.

At the end of the letter, I prayed for the teenager and his mother. I prayed for his soul and salvation. I prayed that God would forgive him for hurting His precious child (ME)! I prayed that God would help the teenager's mother to navigate life without blaming herself for her son's behavior. I prayed for God to protect them both. Moreover, I prayed that God would prevent him from harming other children.

Writing the letter was a very beneficial coping tool to bring me to the place of releasing my anger, hurt, pain, rage, emptiness, and loneliness. Whenever negative emotions surfaced within me, I wrote. Doing so gave me a breakthrough! It freed me, allowing my positive emotions to grow. I rejoiced at being happy, loved, and loving self and others. Armed with this step, I was more determined than ever to be whole.

Acceptance led me to a place of peace and joy, for I was finally able to feel positive emotions internally. I could truly rejoice at the hearing of good news. Acceptance allowed me to know me and know God more intimately; therefore, I was blessed to finally acknowledge my self-worth.

# Chapter 3

# ACKNOWLEDGING YOUR SELF-WORTH

I n the beginning of the book, I mentioned I was focused on being healed and made whole. I knew if the women at the women's retreat were able to survive their stolen innocence, I was worthy of that as well. If the husband at the church where I was attending group counseling sessions was able to be delivered from his dark past so he could love his wife like Christ, I knew I was worthy of that, too. If God healed them, He would heal me as well. I channeled all of my energy into acknowledging and knowing my self-worth.

I remembered one of the women at the retreat referring to herself as a Proverbs 31 Woman. I'd never heard of that saying and longed to know more about it. After reading Proverbs 31:10-31 (see insert below), I understood, for God used that to reveal to me my self-worth as a woman. In spite of what happened to me early in my life, God wants me to know that I am full of worth. I am priceless. I am virtuous. Furthermore, this passage inspired me to no longer harbored low self-esteem or lack self-confidence.

The description of a Proverbs 31 Woman became the very catalyst I needed to know the value of my inner and outer beauty. Looking into a mirror no longer frightens me. Now, it is my favorite thing to do. It reminds me of the laudable metamorphosis I went through to acknowledge, know, and understand my self-worth. The mirror allows me to see myself through God's eyes; beautiful!

I encourage every woman who is reading this book to pray this passage frequently. This habit permitted me to overcome low self-esteem and unworthiness, which were birthed the day the rape occurred. I went through life collecting and believing the negative labels men tried to affix to my soul, especially the searing ones when they could not have their way with me. I was called the "B" word (Hmm sir, I have two legs, not four!), "ugly" (Whatever! You are mad I rejected you!), "gap band member" (Why? You really admire the naturally beautiful gap in my smile!), "fat" (Excuse me sir, I am thick!), "tar baby" (Really! Don't hate on my smooth, silky dark skin!), "mean" (I'm stern!), and "bougie" (Nope, just blessed!). Now I laugh and rebuke negativity when it comes my way. I joyously reject male mess offered to control me. Bye Felicia!

Because of my newfound appraisal of my worth, I am able to compliment others as often as I do. Knowing first-hand the harm and emotional damage I experienced from men I rejected, I avoid speaking negatively about people. I realize that hurting people hurt others. Showering people with words of affection and appreciation affords me the opportunity to speak life into their souls. I offer them the blessed bricks to build the foundation of their self esteem, self confidence, and self-worth.

As a survivor, I empower you to know your self-worth. If God says you are virtuous, it does not matter what others say. It does not matter what has happened in your past. It does not matter how you view yourself. If God says it, then that is all that matters. His Word is true and never fails.

### Proverbs 31:10-31 The Message (MSG)

### Hymn to a Good Wife

> A good woman is hard to find,
>     and worth far more than diamonds.
> Her husband trusts her without reserve,
>     and never has reason to regret it.

Never spiteful, she treats him generously
    all her life long.
She shops around for the best yarns and cottons,
    and enjoys knitting and sewing.
She's like a trading ship that sails to faraway places
    and brings back exotic surprises.
She's up before dawn, preparing breakfast
    for her family and organizing her day.
She looks over a field and buys it,
    then, with money she's put aside, plants a garden.
First thing in the morning, she dresses for work,
    rolls up her sleeves, eager to get started.
She senses the worth of her work,
    is in no hurry to call it quits for the day.
She's skilled in the crafts of home and hearth,
    diligent in homemaking.
She's quick to assist anyone in need,
    reaches out to help the poor.
She doesn't worry about her family when it snows;
    their winter clothes are all mended and ready to wear.
She makes her own clothing,
    and dresses in colorful linens and silks.
Her husband is greatly respected
    when he deliberates with the city fathers.
She designs gowns and sells them,
    brings the sweaters she knits to the dress shops.
Her clothes are well-made and elegant,
    and she always faces tomorrow with a smile.
When she speaks she has something worthwhile to say,
    and she always says it kindly.
She keeps an eye on everyone in her household,
    and keeps them all busy and productive.
Her children respect and bless her;
    her husband joins in with words of praise:
"Many women have done wonderful things,
    but you've outclassed them all!"
Charm can mislead and beauty soon fades.

> The woman to be admired and praised
> is the woman who lives in the Fear-of-God.
> Give her everything she deserves!
> Festoon her life with praises!

There is another passage I prayed daily to better understand my self-worth; Psalm 139:13-16 (see insert below). To know that God formed and covered me increased my knowledge of how valuable I was. To know that I was fearfully and wonderfully made and described as marvelous were major boasts to my self-confidence, self-esteem, and of course, my self-worth.

### Psalm 139:13-16 The Message (MSG)

> Oh yes, you shaped me first inside, then out;
> you formed me in my mother's womb.
> I thank you, High God—you're breathtaking!
> Body and soul, I am marvelously made!
> I worship in adoration—what a creation!
> You know me inside and out,
> you know every bone in my body;
> You know exactly how I was made, bit by bit,
> how I was sculpted from nothing into something.
> Like an open book, you watched me grow from conception to birth;
> all the stages of my life were spread out before you,
> The days of my life all prepared
> before I'd even lived one day.

By meditating on Proverbs 31:10-31 and Psalm 139:13-16, I was able to acknowledge my self-worth. These scriptures reminded me that I was virtuous, fearfully and wonderfully made, and marvelous in his eyes. If God said it, then it was true. If God saw me that way, I deserved to see myself the same way. These attributes prompted me to acquire a new outlook on life as I continued to survive my stolen innocence.

# Chapter 4

# ACQUIRING NEW OUTLOOK

C ompleting the two-year, group counseling sessions was instru-
mental in opening my eyes to the truth. During and after the
program, I continued to use my coping tools of admitting there was
a problem, accepting the problem existed, and acknowledging my
self-worth. I was now ready to acquire a new outlook on me.

As a result of the rape, I saw men as the enemy. I saw myself as
an ugly woman who would never be happy. I saw life through foggy,
dark lenses. I perceived the world and any event in it in a negative
way. In truth, I saw the glass as half empty, never half full. Recalling
the wonderful stories I heard during counseling, I knew it was time
for me to change my vision of self, others, and God. A new outlook
on life was a vital part of my survival from stolen innocence.

To do this, I mediated, studied, and prayed God's words daily.
The more I did so, the closer I grew to God. The closer I felt to Him,
the clearer my vision of Him was made known. As this cycle pro-
gressed, I eventually gained a better, positive perspective on my life.

Below are some scriptures that helped me acquire a new outlook.
They are advantageous as well as comforting. Recite and pray them
as often as needed to change your view of self, others, and God. Life
through God's outlook is positive, refreshing, rewarding, hopeful,
and peaceful.

## Outlook: Do not be afraid...The Lord will fight for you.

Exodus 14:13-14 (NKJV)

13 And Moses said to the people, "Do not be afraid. Stand still, and see the salvation of the Lord, which He will accomplish for you today. For the Egyptians whom you see today, you shall see again no more forever. 14 The Lord will fight for you, and you shall hold your peace."

## Outlook: You are a holy people...keep His commandments.

Deuteronomy 7:6-9 (NKJV)

6 "For you are a holy people to the Lord your God; the Lord your God has chosen you to be a people for Himself, a special treasure above all the peoples on the face of the earth. 7 The Lord did not set His love on you nor choose you because you were more in number than any other people, for you were the least of all peoples; 8 but because the Lord loves you, and because He would keep the oath which He swore to your fathers, the Lord has brought you out with a mighty hand, and redeemed you from the house of bondage, from the hand of Pharaoh king of Egypt. 9 "Therefore know that the Lord your God, He is God, the faithful God who keeps covenant and mercy for a thousand generations with those who love Him and keep His commandments...

## Outlook: No need to fight...The battle is the Lord's.

2 Chronicles 20:15 (NKJV)

And he said, "Listen, all you of Judah and you inhabitants of Jerusalem, and you, King Jehoshaphat! Thus says the LORD to you: 'Do not be afraid nor dismayed because of this great multitude, for the battle *is* not yours, but God's.'"

## Outlook: The Lord is your Shepherd...Dwell in the house of the Lord forever.

Psalm 23 (NKJV)

1 The Lord is my shepherd;

I shall not want.

2 He makes me to lie down in green pastures;

He leads me beside the still waters.

3 He restores my soul;

He leads me in the paths of righteousness

For His name's sake.

4 Yea, though I walk through the valley of the shadow of death,

I will fear no evil;

For You are with me;

Your rod and Your staff, they comfort me.

5 You prepare a table before me in the presence of my enemies;

You anoint my head with oil;

My cup runs over.

6 Surely goodness and mercy shall follow me

All the days of my life;

And I will dwell in the house of the Lord

Forever.

## Outlook: God removed our transgressions....He knows our frame.

Psalm 102:12-14 (NKJV)

12 But You, O Lord, shall endure forever,

And the remembrance of Your name to all generations.

13 You will arise and have mercy on Zion;

For the time to favor her,

Yes, the set time, has come.

14 For Your servants take pleasure in her stones,

And show favor to her dust.

## Outlook: Jesus was wounded....by His stripes we are healed.

Isaiah 53:5 (NKJV)

But He *was* wounded for our transgressions,

*He was* bruised for our iniquities;

The chastisement for our peace *was* upon Him,

And by His stripes we are healed.

**Outlook: The Lord does not change...You are not consumed.**

Malachi 3:6 (NKJV)
For I *am* the LORD, I do not change;
Therefore you are not consumed, O sons of Jacob.

**Outlook: Love your enemies...Your Father in Heaven is perfect.**

Matthew 5:44-48 (NKJV)
44 But I say to you, love your enemies, bless those who curse you, do good to those who hate you, and pray for those who spitefully use you and persecute you, 45 that you may be sons of your Father in heaven; for He makes His sun rise on the evil and on the good, and sends rain on the just and on the unjust. 46 For if you love those who love you, what reward have you? Do not even the tax collectors do the same? 47 And if you greet your brethren only, what do you do more than others? Do not even the tax collectors do so? 48 Therefore you shall be perfect, just as your Father in heaven is perfect.

**Outlook: Whenever you stand praying....forgive your trespasses.**

Mark 11:25-26 (NKJV)
25 "And whenever you stand praying, if you have anything against anyone, forgive him, that your Father in heaven may also forgive you your trespasses. 26 But if you do not forgive, neither will your Father in heaven forgive your trespasses."

**Outlook: Ask and it will be given...give the Holy Spirit to those who ask Him.**

Luke 11:9-13 (NKJV)
9 "So I say to you, ask, and it will be given to you; seek, and you will find; knock, and it will be opened to you. 10 For everyone who asks receives, and he who seeks finds, and to him who knocks it will be opened. 11 If a son asks for bread from any father among you, will he give him a stone? Or if he asks for a fish, will he give him a serpent instead of a fish? 12 Or if he asks for an egg, will he offer him

a scorpion? 13 If you then, being evil, know how to give good gifts to your children, how much more will your heavenly Father give the Holy Spirit to those who ask Him!"

## Outlook: No condemnation....free from the law of sin and death.

Romans 8:1-2 (NKJV)

1 There is therefore now no condemnation to those who are in Christ Jesus, who do not walk according to the flesh, but according to the Spirit. 2 For the law of the Spirit of life in Christ Jesus has made me free from the law of sin and death.

## Outlook: Confess your sins....made unto salvation.

Romans 10:9-10 (NKJV)

9 that if you confess with your mouth the Lord Jesus and believe in your heart that God has raised Him from the dead, you will be saved. 10 For with the heart one believes unto righteousness, and with the mouth confession is made unto salvation.

## Outlook: Present your bodies a living sacrifice...perfect will of God.

Romans 12:1-2 (NKJV).

1 I beseech you therefore, brethren, by the mercies of God, that you present your bodies a living sacrifice, holy, acceptable to God, which is your reasonable service. 2 And do not be conformed to this world, but be transformed by the renewing of your mind, that you may prove what is that good and acceptable and perfect will of God.

## Outlook: If your enemy is hungry...overcome evil with good.

Romans 12:20-21(NKJV)

20 Therefore, "If your enemy is hungry, feed him;

If he is thirsty, give him a drink;

For in so doing you will heap coals of fire on his head." 21 Do not be overcome by evil, but overcome evil with good.

**Outlook: The thief came to steal...Jesus came that we may have life.**

John 10:10 (NKJV)

The thief does not come except to steal, and to kill, and to destroy. I |Jesus| have come that they may have life, and that they may have it more abundantly.

**Outlook: For all the promises of God...anointed us is God.**

2 Corinthians 1:20-21 (NKJV)

20 For all the promises of God in Him are Yes, and in Him Amen, to the glory of God through us. 21 Now He who establishes us with you in Christ and has anointed us is God...

**Outlook: He died for all....ministry of reconciliation.**

2 Corinthians 5:15-18 (NKJV)

15 and He died for all, that those who live should live no longer for themselves, but for Him who died for them and rose again.16 Therefore, from now on, we regard no one according to the flesh. Even though we have known Christ according to the flesh, yet now we know Him thus no longer. 17 Therefore, if anyone is in Christ, he is a new creation; old things have passed away; behold, all things have become new. 18 Now all things are of God, who has reconciled us to Himself through Jesus Christ, and has given us the ministry of reconciliation...

**Outlook: You are a chosen generation....now have obtained mercy.**

1 Peter 2:9-10 (NKJV)

9 But you are a chosen generation, a royal priesthood, a holy nation, His own special people, that you may proclaim the praises of Him who called you out of darkness into His marvelous light; 10 who once were not a people but are now the people of God, who had not obtained mercy but now have obtained mercy.

**Outlook: Confess our sins...Cleanse us from all unrighteousness.**

1 John 1:9 (NKJV)

If we confess our sins, He is faithful and just to forgive us *our* sins and to cleanse us from all unrighteousness.

**Outlook: God will wipe away every tear...he shall be My son.**

Revelations 21:4-7 (NKJV)

4 And God will wipe away every tear from their eyes; there shall be no more death, nor sorrow, nor crying. There shall be no more pain, for the former things have passed away." 5 Then He who sat on the throne said, "Behold, I make all things new." And He said to me, "Write, for these words are true and faithful." 6 And He said to me, "It is done! I am the Alpha and the Omega, the Beginning and the End. I will give of the fountain of the water of life freely to him who thirsts. 7 He who overcomes shall inherit all things, and I will be his God and he shall be My son.

**Outlook: I am coming quickly...the First and the Last.**

Revelations 22:12-13 (NKJV)

12 "And behold, I am coming quickly, and My reward is with Me, to give to everyone according to his work. 13 I am the Alpha and the Omega, the Beginning and the End, the First and the Last."

# Chapter 5

# A NEW DATING LIFE

Now that I had acquired a new outlook on life, I yearned to start work on establishing a healthy dating life. That's right. A dating life! Thanks to the group counseling sessions and my prayer life, I was ready to mingle.

Listening to the women in the group counseling session discuss their marriages and explain how much their healing has allowed them to love their spouses in a more affectionate manner, I knew then I needed to finally address my dating life. My primary objectives for wanting to survive involved my need to cultivate self love, open to intimacy, being in love and loved, and trusting a man with my heart and life. God had given me a desire to love, and now that I was emotionally ready and able to step into this arena, up popped the million dollar question: "Who would I date?" The answer, God. ☺ Gotcha!

After listening to endless stories of surviving stolen innocence, I discovered that most of the women in my counseling group had never dated in the right way. Primarily, they saw men as a savior, never as a friend or lover. They used men because a man had used them. They stole money, trips, and other material things from men to avoid trusting, loving, and committing. I must admit, I, too, never trusted a man with my body or heart for fear of them hurting me. Honestly, I did not know what true love was nor how to love others.

When I did date, I was guarded. I never allowed the men I dated to fully love me or shower me with material things because I feared they would want something in return; sex. I told myself to stay numb and keep them in a friend zone. This defense mechanism prevented me from dating God as well.

For me to rise above my stolen innocence, dating God was the final step. Spending quality, intimate time with God was the last leg of my journey to healing. It led me to being all alone with Him. To ensure I was fully engaged, I chose not to date during this process and became very protective of my dating time with God where family and friends were concerned, also.

With God, I knew He would protect my heart. After all, it is His heart. I knew He was always available to be there for me whenever I needed him. I knew He loved me. I knew He would provide all of my needs. I knew He would fight for me. I knew He was trustworthy, but I had not yet learned to trust God one hundred percent. This would soon change during my courtship with Him.

In 2006, God sent challenges to get me to trust Him wholly. He knew that in order for me to love a man, I had to trust Him with my whole heart so I prayed and rehearsed Proverbs 3:5-8 on a regular basis.

## Proverbs 3:5-8 New King James Version (NKJV)

5 Trust in the Lord with all your heart,
And lean not on your own understanding;
6 In all your ways acknowledge Him,
And He shall direct your paths.
7 Do not be wise in your own eyes;
Fear the Lord and depart from evil.
8 It will be health to your flesh,
And strength to your bones.

The trust challenges I faced came one after another. I was unable to catch my breath. The first challenge was leaving a church where I served faithfully for 12 years. Prior to the separation, God prepared me by sending fasting instructions and surrounding me with prayer partners who were not members of that church. This was the beginning of me trusting God again. I had to position myself to allow new people to speak into my life and pray for and with me.

One of the pray partners told me that I did not trust God and this upcoming time in my life would bring me to a place of absolute trust in Him. To get to this place, I needed to forgive God. I had not forgiven God for allowing my innocence to be stolen or for taking my biological father from me early in my life.

I pondered on those words from my new prayer partner repeatedly. Each time this came to my memory, I cried uncontrollably. I realized I had unforgiveness in my heart towards God. I forgave the young teenage boy. I forgave myself, but I had not forgiven God for allowing that day to happen.

I remembered asking God to forgive me for not forgiving Him. I asked almost every day for a year. I wanted to make sure I was not walking in unforgiveness, especially against the One who created me. Eventually, one of my prayer partners called me to say that God had forgiven me for not asking or forgiving Him. At the hearing of this amazing news, a wave of joy rushed through my body. I was so relieved.

In June 2008, I received God's instructions for me to transition from being gainfully employed to being a full-time graduate student. Who does that in their 30s? Me, I suppose. Whatever it took for me to fully trust and date God, I was ready. God used daily inspirational messages, two co-workers, and new prayer partners to confirm the request to quit my job.

But this request was a leap of faith indeed. I had no other job lined up. No savings. No means of providing for my living needs.

All types of fears rose up in my spirit. I convinced myself that this was clearly not of God. I fasted and prayed, seeking answers, for I knew God would not have me to risk my good credit, release my new car or the new house He'd just given me. What was God really asking of me? And, was this task of God?

To make sure I understood and was well prepared for this enormous trust test, God positioned me to watch television one night. Mike Murdock was speaking about radical faith on the Trinity Broadcasting Network (TBN) Channel. He said someone was being asked to do an uncommon thing to obtain uncommon favor with God, and it required radical faith. I laughed aloud. Then, I cried louder. Not to tell anyone until God said so was my next instruction. No family, no friends, no one.

As I was processing this message from Mike Murdock, I asked God why I should not tell anyone. Then Mike Murdock answered that question as well. He said you have not trusted anyone in your life since you were young, including God. In order to go higher in God, trust is required. Ouch! Talk about quick responses.

Needless to say, I immediately informed my employer that as of September 2008, I was leaving the company to become a full-time graduate student at Strayer University. I was leaving a full-time position with a computer company in a Level 2 Help Desk Technical Support position to become a full-time graduate student at Strayer University to study Public Administration. When the owner of the company and I met, he asked me if I was going to work for another employer. I repeatedly told him I was not. This was a leap of faith that required me to place my complete trust in God. He understood, since he, too, was a Christian of radical faith.

The third trust challenge was financial. Between June and September 2008, I had no time to store savings. Furthermore, with a new car and house, there were no savings. And, lastly, being single, I had no husband to rely on. I had to trust God for my every need, and He met my every need. My courtship with God was getting off to a fabulous start, and everything seemed to be moving at a fast pace.

For the next year, I did not work a full-time job. As a matter of fact, God instructed me to volunteer with a local domestic violence non-profit. The owner was a survivor of stolen innocence as well. Her first husband physically and emotionally abused her for 15 years, during her tenure as a pastor of a church. God was teaming me with kindred spirits with amazing testimonies; for, I, too, had survived a domestically violent relationship.

I met many survivors, who were mainly foreigners, at this non-profit. The humility and gratitude these women and children displayed touched my heart. I watched them daily rejoicing, knowing they had a safe haven. They were protected from their abusers. Most importantly, the resources they received helped them to start a better life. These participants inspired me to finish my courtship with God strong.

My house and credit score comprised the fourth challenge. After I had not made a mortgage payment in over a year, the lender began the foreclosure process. In addition, a crooked collection agency filed a frivolous lawsuit against me and threatened garnishment. On top of that, the auto and credit card lender were threatening to repossess my car and freeze my credit card. When I was done convincing the lenders and creditors that I would remit payment as soon as possible, I surrendered to God.

I threw up my hands and echoed throughout my house as loud as possible, "God, You win! I give my heart and mind to You one hundred percent. I trust You to provide with all my heart. Not my will be done, but Yours be done. The house, the car, my credit, and my life all belong to You anyway. You are my Shepherd, I shall not want. I will not worry about tomorrow. Help me to get through this day. Send help now."

After I finished proclaiming to God my commitment to trust Him totally, I fell to the floor and began worshipping and praising Him. I asked for peace of mind, and, in my heart, I asked for strength throughout this process. Moreover, I asked God to continue to order my steps.

Within the days following my surrender, God ceased all collections. Money flowed from the north, south, east, and west from various sources and people. A newfound level of trust, peace, rest, and joy entered my heart, life, and home. God showed me the rewards of trusting Him.

In that pivotal moment of my dating life with God, trust was no longer my issue. Everything the enemy had stolen from me since childhood, God restored. Peace and security in my home were restored. I was able to rest. I stopped worrying. My faith in God to provide all of my needs was unshakable. I was a survivor.

I realized how the stolen innocence had impacted my trust in God. I equated this vile act with God letting me down. In my heart, God was not trustworthy anymore, and I could not say I trusted God. I did not trust anyone, especially men with my heart. Dating God was the start of me reaping a secured level of trust in Him.

Restoration was the last trust challenge. God needed me to have faith in Him to restore me fully. Thanks to the group counseling sessions, God had restored me emotionally. When the dust cleared from all the trust challenges, God caused an immediate restoration to occur, and the degree to which God restored me was astonishing.

The first restoration occurred in November 2011 when God saved the house from foreclosure. I rejoiced knowing I had a safe, peaceful place to lay my head nightly without the fearful possibility of homelessness. The second restoration was in February 2012. God opened the door for me to gain full-time employment with excellent benefits and a salary greater than the one I walked away from in 2008. Joyfully, I realized my newly redeemed finances were more than enough to bring past-due bills current and making payments in full and on time. During my unemployment period, I was unable to make full or partial payments, which caused my credit score to plummet more than 20 points, but my God had a bigger plan; credit restoration.

Now that I was in good standing on my financial obligations, God instructed me to purchase a new car, since my car began consistently failing in route to my new job. In February 2013, God blessed me with a brand-new 2013 Nissan Altima 3.6 SV. I was the first owner. To make certain every car note was paid in full and on time, God allowed me to receive a pay raise. As it relates to my credit restoration, God did not permit me to seek a credit repair company. For two to three years after I left my job, in 2008, every negative mark the creditors reported to the credit bureaus stayed on my credit report, preventing me from securing credit cards and loans. I was denied credit on a monthly basis. Though a little discouraged, I was grateful for my steady income, which was more than enough to allow me to resume making timely payments to all my creditors, and I even fully paid off two credit cards. Miraculously, my credit score increased over 20 points, proving there was no loss. Ain't my date good? God does it all the time. Restoration was mine, I was feeling good, and I was too blessed to be stressed and depressed.

A new dating life with God brought me closer to Him. I was able to truly trust Him again, which is an ongoing process. I learned God would never fail me and would ever provide all of my needs. Lastly, God showed me how strong I was during our courtship.

My will power to enter into a place of healing was untouch-able. My faith went from being small to radical. There was no one or nothing to keep me from trusting God. Opening to leaps of faith amazed and impressed me. My self-worth was more valuable than it had ever been.

Upon completing this remarkable relationship with God, I was now ready for a relationship. I was emotionally available to love another man and receive his love, for I had the tools I needed to build a relationship. I felt like a Proverbs 31 Woman who knew her virtue.

After dating the most available, worthiest, and wealthiest pow-erhouse I know, God, my perception of a healthy date life changed dramatically. My dating life before this life- changing experience consisted of me looking for a man to fill a void left from the absence of my father and the rape. My understanding of love was severely flawed. I'd made myself available for unworthy becks and calls. I rearranged my schedule for a man. I trusted men's empty words, only to discover webs of lies. As long as a man provided affection and some type of security, I felt he loved me. Was I ever wrong!

My real date, God, had taught me about real love. He laid it out so elegantly in 1 Corinthians 13: 4-10 (see insert below). These words came alive in my soul. Today, if a man displays the opposite of this Godly Love, I quickly dismiss him, no longer able to tolerate specious love. I know real love now. God has healed me of the false idea of love. He healed me from stolen innocence. Equipped with God's love and peace, I am able to enjoy a healthy dating life now, and I encourage you to know this love.

## 1 Corinthians 13:4-10 New King James Version (NKJV)

4 Love suffers long and is kind; love does not envy; love does not parade itself, is not puffed up; 5 does not behave rudely, does not seek its own, is not provoked, thinks no evil; 6 does not rejoice in iniquity, but rejoices in the truth; 7 bears all things, believes all things, hopes all things, endures all things.

8 Love never fails. But whether there are prophecies, they will fail; whether there are tongues, they will cease; whether there is knowledge, it will vanish away. 9 For we know in part and we

prophesy in part. 10 But when that which is perfect has come, then that which is in part will be done away.

Dating God was the finale to surviving stolen innocence. Establishing a deep-rooted level of trust for God was major for me. The devil tried to taint my view of God by filling my mind with lies about God failing me. To God be the glory, He had a bigger and better plan for my life. Having the will power and determination to build a healthy relationship with God was the motivation I needed to stay focused and break free of my self-imposed prison.

Just in case you are wondering if I am dating one man exclusively at this time, I am not. Dating, I am, and it feels great. When it is time, God will reveal the mate He has for me. My daily prayer is for God to open my chosen mate's eyes and heart to see my worth and to love me like God does, forever and unconditionally.

# Chapter 6

## CONCLUSION

At the time of this writing, November 2015, I am still rejoicing, knowing I survived. Throughout my life, I have met many people, men and women, who have experienced situations similar to what happened to me. Some of these people were Christians. Some were of a different faith. Some were pastors, ministers, deacons, or leaders in their church homes.

Some of the women I met admitted that as a result of their stolen innocence, they became promiscuous or opened to same-sex relationships. Because of anger, insecurities, and trust issues, some women adopted celibacy. To my surprise, some of the men vouchsafed similar admissions. In light of this awareness of what could happen as a result of survivors having physically overcome a situation of stolen innocence, I want the world to know that regardless of your gender, religion, sexual orientation or race, your survival is a blessing. Like me, though, you must decide to not only survive, you must thrive. You must learn to love again, embracing the God within you so that you can fully experience well being and agape love in the world.

Use the steps of admission, acceptance, acknowledgment of your self-worth, acquiring a new outlook on life, and dating God to begin your survival process. You are more than worthy of it.

I pray you found this book to be a blessing. If so, please share it with others. You never know who needs a way of escape.

Moreover, I pray you were empowered to face the person who took your precious or sacred thing from you against your will. I pray you were able to finally share your experience. Sharing is a form of releasing the embarrassment or guilt as a result of such a violation. I pray God leads you to a group counseling session or to a skilled counselor or therapist to aid in your healing.

**Although your innocence was stolen,
you are worthy to survive and thrive!**

# Encouraging Words

Dear Friends,

I pray my surviving stolen innocence has been the motivation you need to start your own journey. As you heal from your past, please share your testimony with me. I can be contacted via e-mail at aliciab_speaks@gmail.com. I would love to hear your testimony. I am available for speaking engagements as well and can be contacted at the same e-mail address.

Before I depart, I leave you the encouraging words below. I pray God lays healing hands upon you to remove all the hurt and pain embedded in your hearts and minds. Each day, you will gain the strength to press forward. You got this. Victory is yours.

## Philippians 3:12-14 The Message (MSG)

Focus on the Goal

I'm not saying that I have this all together, that I have it made. But I am well on my way, reaching out for Christ, who has so wondrously reached out for me. Friends, don't get me wrong: By no means do I count myself an expert in all of this, but I've got my eye on the goal, where God is beckoning us onward—to Jesus. I'm off and running and I'm not turning back.

Thanks for your support!
Alicia L. Brown
aliciab.speaks@gmail.com

CPSIA information can be obtained at www.ICGtesting.com
Printed in the USA
LVOW08s2024220416

484937LV00002B/18/P